BEYOND
PHYSICAL
MATTER

BEYOND PHYSICAL MATTER

A MOTIVATE ENTERPRISE PRODUCTION

WWW.MOTIVATEENTERPRISE.COM

©**2024 MOTIVATE ENTERPRISE INC.**

All rights reserved. Printed in the United States of America.

No part of this publication may be reproduced, stored in a retrieval system, or transmitted in any form or by any means, electronic, mechanical, photocopying, recording, or otherwise without the written permission of the publisher.

ME, its logos and marks are trademarks of Motivate Enterprise, Inc.

ISBN: 979-8-218-48548-1

For additional copies of this book or bulk orders,
Contact: www.motivateenterprise.com/contact-us

INTRODUCTION

Imagine walking along an expansive beach at sunrise, listening to the waves lapping against the shore as they come in and go out… with the powerful, natural movement of ebb and flow.

Picture a crystal-clear night sky, filled with millions of stars, each trying to outshine the next.

Envision every aspect of nature's glorious beauty, from sturdy oak trees to wispy, weeping willows, from living beings as tiny as a ladybug to the massive elephant, and from rushing rivers to vast mountain lakes.

Or contemplate the miracle of life itself!

As magnificent as these wonders are, is it possible that there is something that goes *beyond physical matter?*

As glorious as this physical world is… filled with magical beauty and splendor… there's something that goes beyond physical matter. We call it quantum physics or quantum mechanics. These are things that our physical eyes can't see, but our human spirit can sense.

I invite you to take a journey with me as we explore the world that exists ***beyond physical matter.***

- Sir Don Boyer

"What you think, you become. What you feel, you attract. What you imagine, you create."

- Buddha

TABLE OF CONTENTS

CHAPTER ONE 11
  PHYSICS

CHAPTER TWO 25
  LIGHT & SOUND

CHAPTER THREE 37
  VIBRATIONS

CHAPTER FOUR 51
  PAST TRAUMA

CHAPTER FIVE 63
  SUCCESS

CHAPTER SIX 71
  AWAKENING

"Change your conception of yourself and you will automatically change the world in which you live. Do not try to change people; they are only messengers telling you who you are. Revalue yourself and they will confirm the change."

- Neville Goddard

PHYSICS
CHAPTER ONE

"In any given moment, we have two options:
to step forward into growth or to step back
into safety."

- Abraham Maslow

"Life is either a daring adventure or
nothing at all."

- Helen Keller

"You are never too old to set another goal or
to dream a new dream.'"

- C.S. Lewis

PHYSICS

Physics helps us to make new discoveries, though those discoveries often bring with them new questions. This perspective of physics often focuses on what we already know versus what we *will know* in the future. It's exciting and constantly moving.

PRACTICAL PHYSICS

Practical physics is a collection of experiments that demonstrate physical concepts and processes. It is the science of matter, motion, and energy.

We take elements we can define or measure, pure facts, and consider what is real and what is possible if we experiment with these elements.

QUANTUM MECHANICS

Quantum mechanics goes beyond practical physics. It is the branch of physics that deals with the behavior of particles

- matter and light - on the atomic and subatomic scale. It relates to the properties of molecules and atoms. Understanding the nature and behavior of matter and energy on these small scales helps us to understand energy and the uncertainties of life.

You don't have to be a scientist or physicist to understand how a basic understanding of physics and energy can influence your life positively.

The experts in **BEYOND PHYSICAL MATTER** have come together to share their thoughts on physics in a whole new way… so you can apply the laws of physics to achieve a more fulfilling and satisfying life.

Baroness Dr. Kara Scott Dently

Practical physics is what we know as Newtonian physics, where you're looking at forces, what they use when they're in a collision, what is the weight capacity when you're sitting on a chair and appreciating the weight load. These are things that we can actually physically measure.

These are the things that we cannot see. More people now are starting to dig deeper into quantum physics because they're starting to see that there is more than what meets our physical senses.

Dr. Steve Schwartz

But if we go deeper than that, we're looking into quantum physics, which works with potentiality, and waves, and particles…

Morley Robbins

First, we have to understand what quantum physics is. My favorite book that I've ever read was *The Tao of Physics*. What impressed me the most about that book was that these were several world-renowned physicists talking about the Tao of physics… the inner game of physics… the quantum dimension of physics, was their unassailable belief in God.

Sir James Gray Robinson, Esq.

There were some important discoveries in quantum physics about a hundred years ago that totally revolutionized the world. And there was a huge shift of consciousness in the early 1900s.

Napoleon Hill was an expert and a master of mental energy. Albert Einstein was a quantum physics genius who figured out how these little subatomic particles worked. Tesla was an expert and a master of electromagnetic energy. All of these men agreed on one thing… whatever we perceive as matter is not real: it's all energy.

Jason Estes

So, quantum physics is the study of the quantum world and how it affects the physical world. That's the best way I can describe it to the layman. It goes very deep, but it's all theoretical. You can't really explain quantum because to explain quantum, you have to be able to understand malleable time, which is outside of time itself. And we still very much exist inside of time. We're theorizing from the inside out what it would be like to be outside of time.

Sir Dr. Antoine Chevalier

It looks like, finally, science and religion now are going to be able to somehow connect, and quantum physics is the bridge right now. To me, that's very exciting.

"The measure of intelligence is the ability to change."

- Albert Einstein

"What the mind of man can conceive and believe, it can achieve."

- Napoleon Hill

"What we achieve inwardly will change outer reality."

- Plutarch

THE CONCEPT OF ENERGY

Sir Don Boyer

In this world of energy, if we can't smell it… if we can't hear it… nor touch it, where is it? How can we contact that which is invisible or that which the physical senses cannot detect?

The ancient civilizations called this the outer world and the inner world. The outer world is the physical substance that we can touch and to which our five senses can relate. Where is the inner world?

The inner world is our thoughts, our beliefs, and our vibrations. These are the frequencies that we emit every time we think a thought. Our inner world is the realm of creation, and the physical world is the realm of effects. If we think it, we can have it, because it will show up in the physical realm. We can't say that we can *feel* our thoughts, but we know that they're real. This is why we say quantum physics is going *beyond physical matter*.

John Assaraf

When we are born, we're pretty much born a clean slate… other than any genetic predispositions. The part that is not built in is our belief system. As we experience the world, we begin to give meanings to things. We learn from our parents, our teachers, and our experiences. The meanings we give things boils down to the fact that we become conditioned. So, we don't end up seeing the world as *it is*, but rather we end up seeing the world through our lens of what we've learned about how the world is.

Baroness Dr. Kara Scott Dently

There is no shortage of information and knowledge available, so what we want to do is open up our thought processes and possibilities, because we're all potential energy just waiting for everything that is in us to come out.

H.E. Baron Dr. John Sachtouras

Most of us are curious about energy and want to understand how it works and what it means. Many of us read about it, hoping to gain a greater knowledge about energy. I've personally read countless books, but it didn't mean anything until I became self-aware of understanding what energy is about.

There is nothing more important in life than to see the Universe, to recognize that there is energy everywhere, and to feel grateful for that understanding. The Universal energy is everywhere and is available to everyone.

Jason Estes

When you see energy and understand energy, you're unlocking your reticular activating system. This is the thing in your brain that's telling you what you can see. This is the wildest thing about us!

We literally tend to censor everything we see at a core level, before we even process a reality or determine what it is.

> **The higher your energy level,**
> **the more efficient your body.**
> **The more efficient your body,**
> **the better you feel and the more**
> **you will use your talent to produce**
> **outstanding results.**
>
> - Tony Robbins

John Assaraf

Everything is energy, whether it's the radio station that you're listening to, that is a radio frequency; it's energy. If it's light coming from the sun, it's energy. Even the feelings that you have put out an energetic field.

Sir James Gray Robinson, Esq.

Energy is the building block of what we perceive is reality. Energy brings life into the universe.

Szilard Dosa

Everything is energy. We are energy. Everything in the Universe is energy. When we look at the physical matter, we see that beyond that physical matter is energy.

Sir Dr. Antoine Chevalier

The energy and the physical world are intertwined; we can't really separate them. We perceive physical reality as solid, but it's an energy field, just like the others. It's just like our five senses. So whatever energy field we are experiencing through the physical reality is being perceived as physical, because of our five senses.

Jeremy Hoffmann

The way I like to describe energy is that it's the language of life, although not everyone is aware that they are speaking. I believe energy is everything, it's constant, it is moving through us, it is moving around us, it is all things, and it cannot be destroyed.

Positive emotional energy is the key to health, happiness, and wellbeing. The more positive you are, the better your life will be in every area.

- Brian Tracy

Morley Robbins

Energy brings the body to life. Energy is what enables thousands and thousands of chemical transactions to take place. The concept of energy and life are flip sides of the same coin. If you don't have energy, you don't have life.

Barbie Layton

So, in our world, we have the physical energy that the body needs to function, but then there's also the spiritual energy as well. And, in this frame, this is the most important part because it's the place of where you get to go beyond… you get to go play with the Universe.

Sir Don Boyer

This energy, this fundamental entity of nature, is all around. Its power is in us and runs through us. Its presence is everywhere we go and in everything we do. This is what makes the existence of energy and quantum physics so powerful.

As we start to expand our mind and expand our energy, we begin to get a glimpse into understanding life. We're not put here on this Earth for a short period of time just to live out an existence. We were designed for greatness! We were designed to achieve, to expand, to explore, and to contribute.

Unfortunately, most of us have been conditioned to believe that we are limited. So, if we have this unlimited power at our disposal… if you and I have the ability to create that which we think to become real in this physical realm, how do we do it? How is it that we are able to harness that power and intentionally bring it into our physical realm?

> **"Your life does not get better by chance.
> It gets better by change."**
>
> - Jim Rohn

"The purpose of life is not to be happy. It is to be useful, to be honorable, to be compassionate, to have it make some difference that you have lived and lived well."

- Ralph Waldo Emerson

LIGHT & SOUND
CHAPTER TWO

"There is a time when one must decide either to risk everything to fulfill one's dreams or sit for the rest of one's life in the backyard."

- Earl Nightingale

"The mind is everything. What you think, you become."

- Buddha

"Nothing comes from without, all things come from within – from the subconscious."

- Neville Goddard

LIGHT & SOUND

Barbie Layton

The whole entire world is energy, vibration, and frequency. So, if you look at that from the perspective of light and sound, it's something that is universal and that anybody can tap into.

The most exciting part it is understanding that everybody has the ability to tap into the quantum field.

Dr. Milton Howard Jr.

You have light on one level and you have sound on another level. Those are spaces of energy that are constantly moving towards definition.

So, light and sound give us the opportunity for definition. Our ideas impact sound… and sound emerges to become something. This gives us a power through our ideas to define anything that we want to define for our future.

Dr. Steve Schwartz

The difference between light and sound is speed. As we begin to slow down, the light… it grounds into sound.

"The universe is change; our life is what our thoughts make it."

- Marcus Aurelius

THINK

Sir James Gray Robinson, Esq.

This is what I believe, from a very close connection with God… "Think it and make it so."

Baroness Dr. Kara Scott Dently

Much of what we see in the physical world was originally just in someone's imagination.

Szilard Dosa

We each have our own energy… and we can direct it. When we have a purpose in our life, it's important to apply our imagination to it because this is a faculty of what the mind can create. This purpose and creation are what we should focus on.

We need to hold in our minds our intention… what we want to create in our lives… what kind of state we want to be in, and then keep our eyes open and be always be aware of our intentions.

Don't give up. Simply start with where you are, think about a purpose, and try to think of what you need to achieve what you want… piece by piece, little by little. Just follow your intuition and stay focused on what you want.

Attila Balazs

I find it's important for every person to have a desire, have a dream… and have a value system to follow. And, what someone expects from others or from life itself, be willing to do it a similar way for himself or herself. This is because we can only expect from others that which we're willing to do ourselves.

Dr. Milton Howard Jr.

Having a purpose in life and designing that purpose is one of the most extreme privileges we have of being a human being.

> **"A goal is a dream with a deadline."**
>
> - Napoleon Hill

SPEAK

Baroness Dr. Kara Scott Dently

It is critical that we understand how all these things are interconnected… and that we are mindful of the words that we say. A person might say, "I don't say anything negative; I don't allow anything negative to come out of my mouth."

But what we *think* is even more important. Our subconscious mind speaks to us *all the time!* So just because you may not speak a negative thought out loud, think about what are you saying to yourself. What are you thinking? Remember that your subconscious mind is always listening to your thoughts as well as your words.

H.E. Baron Dr. John Sachtouras

We are the only beings who talk to ourselves silently. We're the only ones who can actually program our body and mind. Every word has energy. The word itself can heal you or destroy you. We destroy our own health with the wrong words. We destroy our health and our environment and relationships because words come from an emotion and thinking process. Once you understand what kind of energy words can have, magic will happen in your life.

Morley Robbins

One of the most powerful experiences I had was learning the importance of words and to be able to choose the right words. We have this ultimate control over our destiny because of the words we choose to use because they do, in fact, empower us.

Szilard Dosa

When we say something, this is a creation; this is when the energy becomes physical matter; this is the first physical creation of our thinking process. So, your analytical… your logical mind is created to be the guard at the gate of your subconscious mind.

> **You are the master of your destiny.**
> **You can influence, direct,**
> **and control your own environment.**
> **You can make your life what you want it to be.**
>
> - Napoleon Hill

FEEL

Baroness Dr. Kara Scott Dently

Sometimes we can have thoughts like, "I don't want that to happen." Don't put any emotion behind it. If I have a thought that I *don't* want to manifest or to come true, I take it out of my body and keep it in my head so that I'm not feeling any fear. I don't want to be thinking, "Oh my God, what if *that* happens?" The self-talk is part of it, but it's the emotion that you put behind it.

Jason Estes

If you bring energy into a situation, what you're doing is you're amplifying that situation. Whatever it is, if you're upset and you're bringing energy into the situation, congratulations, you just amplified that you're upset! But if you're happy, you're amplifying that happiness. So, when you're amplifying that, that's really just energy. If you want to amplify your feeling, you're able to expand that feeling out, right? And that's a beautiful space because now you can reflect on it and understand it. But when you're emoting, you're pushing that on other people, no matter whether it's happiness, joy, anger, resentment… it doesn't matter. You're pushing that.

H.E. Baron Dr. John Sachtouras

Whatever we say, it comes from a thinking process to an emotional connection from heart. That emotion encapsulates energy inside. And the better you feel, the more you talk to yourself, your body will react amazingly.

"To be yourself in a world that is constantly trying to make you something else is the greatest accomplishment."

- Ralph Waldo Emerson

"Your time is limited; don't waste it living someone else's life."

- Steve Jobs

"What lies behind us and what lies before us are tiny matters compared to what lies within us."

- Ralph Waldo Emerson

"We are not human beings on a spiritual journey. We are spiritual beings on a human journey."

- Stephen R. Covey

VIBRATIONS
CHAPTER THREE

VIBRATIONS

Eric Zehnder

The model we have had for all these centuries past has been like, "If you study the piano really well, not the player, you study the piano. Okay?" That's how standard physics works. And so the whole notion was, "What humans bring to it doesn't matter. It's a piano, for God's sake! It has these structures; it makes these notes."

So, imagine instead you say, "Wow… wait a minute. Yeah, knowing the piano is something, but how the *human person plays the piano* is actually crucial to the reality we get."

Oh my… I think what we're saying here is think of the responsibility to human beings… if you are somehow calling into being the song, the reality.

> **The quantum reality in you is greater than the circumstances around you.**
>
> - Eric Zehnder

Jeremy Hoffmann

Energy, creative ideas, these are all thoughts. We could call them a vision. We call people visionaries who have these incredible ideas. But it's not actually tangibly physically real in this dimension until that thought comes down through the human form. When we use our words, not only are we actualizing these into reality, but we are also giving context. We are giving form to something that used to be invisible and is now physical. And, depending on how we want to respond to that energy with our thoughts, with our feelings, our beliefs, that creates the reality… that creates the form in which we live our lives.

Morley Robbins

The world as we know it is a mirror of who we are. The beam that we send out comes back to us.

Jason Estes

The part that's so important to understand is that when it comes to the quantum, we are only capable of receiving what we *believe* we can receive. We have the ability to choose what we want to be, and we get to choose what that looks like… our divine intelligence… our spark.

Sir Don Boyer

When we look at this physical world, our physical lives, it

would appear to us and to the natural eye that we are separate beings… that everything is separate and has its own identity. But that is simply an *illusion* of separation because quantum physics tells us that everything is connected in this energetic web called *quantum entanglement*. It helps us to understand that we are not actually separated, but we're unified and we're all one.

> **"There are only two ways to live your life. One is as though nothing is a miracle. The other is as though everything is a miracle.**
>
> - Albert Einstein

Baroness Dr. Kara Scott Dently

Our ability to work with, communicate, and connect with other human beings is on a quantum level.

Szilard Dosa

Everything is connected. Everything in existence has an effect on the energy… its own energy and also of the energy of the Universal field.

John Assaraf

We've all had the experience of walking into a room or talking to somebody that we know is feeling low; something's wrong, and we know something's wrong. We have this intuition that something's wrong. And even when we ask them, "Hey, what's wrong?" They will say, "Oh, nothing." And we will encourage them. "Come on, I know something's wrong." That's *energy.*

We have intuitive faculties of mind as well. We can pick up on the tonality; our brains are always looking for cues. Our brains learn to pick up on the vibe. "He has a great vibe, or she has a terrible vibe," right? Why? *Because we are energetic beings.*

Sir James Gray Robinson, Esq.

We're all connected by energy. We're constantly exchanging energy. And when we read somebody and look at their body language, we pick up on things. We can tell whether or not that person means to harm us or if they're there to help us.

Jeremy Hoffmann

Everything is energy and energy is intrinsically impacting all that we do. There's the physical body and then there's the energetic body. The energetic body is that *invisible* body. Maybe you've an example like this: you have a gut feeling about someone, and there are things happening in your gut. This is simply an energy that you are sensing when you are speaking to someone, or when you walk into a room and meet an individual. That's part of that energetic body that is communicating to you.

The signal from that *energetic body* is moving inside the *physical body* and working with your hormones, your dopamine receptors, your serotonin, to allow you to feel something, allow you to communicate, and allow you to react or respond to a current situation.

> **We become what we think about. Energy flows where attention goes.**
>
> - Rhonda Byrne

Sir James Gray Robinson, Esq.

It's important to understand what kind of energy you're associating with. What kind of energy are you around? Do you allow people who are critical, who are pessimistic, who are never supportive around you? Because that's going to affect the energy that you hold inside your body.

We're like tuning forks. If you take two tuning forks and hit one of them, it will start to vibrate. You can even hear it. Soon, the second one will begin to vibrate, too, even though you haven't hit it.

That's similar to what happens when you're up against somebody who's negative. You're going to start vibrating at a similar level. And, if you're around somebody positive, they're a joy to be with and you'll feel great. They're actually raising your energy… lifting you up.

Barbie Layton

There's always a flip side to everything. If somebody can send positive energy to people, that means that people can send negative energy, as well. This is why your own personal "spiritual hygiene" is so important. You can clear yourself and your energy fields on a regular basis to stay clean and pure.

Attila Balazs

If we have clear thoughts and love controls our actions, then the universe and our life will return to us the same positive energies, positive thoughts.

"Life is really simple, but we insist on making it complicated."

- Confucius

"Life will give you whatever experience is most helpful for the evolution of your consciousness."

- Eckhart Tolle

"Life is not a problem to be solved, but a reality to be experienced."

- Søren Kierkegaard

PHYSICAL ENERGY

Jeremy Hoffmann

I believe that energy can impact the cells, the mitochondria, the DNA. That's my energetic connection to the field of energy that's all around us. It's a matter of the practice that goes into it, the discipline that goes into the question, "How are you going to hold yourself accountable to live in greater alignment?"

When we're in alignment, we're channeling… connecting to energy from beyond our physical bodies, and everything that we do is influencing us. The food that we eat, the people we surround ourselves with, the media that we consume, the water that we drink… all of that is impacting us. All of that is energy.

Dr. Steve Schwartz

Just think from a scale perspective, there are a hundred trillion cells in our bodies. And if we go into one of these hundred trillion cells, we'll see that there are an infinite number of subatomic particles. And if we go in that lowest common denominator, there's a very interesting phenomenon that occurs. It's called a photonic emission. And that is when there is literally a spark, a spark of energy that is released every time an electron bounces from one cell to the next. Our physical expression is made up of infinite numbers of these photonic emissions and it validates that we are actually light.

Sir Don Boyer

Do you realize that the molecular structure, our very cells, are listening to every word that we say? Every time we have a feeling, every time we have an emotion, every time we have a prolonged thought, our cellular structure is impacted. When we begin to think about that, we begin to understand the relationship between health and healing and all the modalities that come together in that arena.

Sir James Gray Robinson, Esq.

Anything that affects our energy will affect our physical bodies. I know that there are many people out there who think that energy healing is a little strange. And there are people that think that modern medicine is the end all/be all answer to everything. But I want to give you a little bit of history because I think it will put into perspective the fact that we're all marching to the same place.

Chinese medicine, oriental medicine, and Ayurvedic medicine all came up with a system that relates to how energy flows through the body in certain paths. They're called meridians. There are also specific points in our body. These are called chakras or vortexes. And each one of these vortexes or chakras has a different effect on a different area of the body. Modern medicine is now proving that these systems were right.

There is a nerve that comes from the cranial nerves that go around our head and skull back to the spinal column and they connect with a nerve that is called the Vagus nerve. And the Vagus nerve goes from the back of your head, all the way down into your legs. The Vagus nerve regulates your organs, your blood pressure, your moods, and the function of all your glands. It's the highway that communicates between the brain and the body.

The most incredible proof is that if you take the endocrine chart and the chakra chart and put them over each other, they are identical matches!

"The unexamined life is not worth living."

- Socrates

Baroness Dr. Kara Scott Dently

Each organ ties into a certain emotion. For instance, when it comes to the heart, things that may disappoint you or people who may have let you down will resonate within your heart with a negative or sad frequency. Many times, when people have liver failure, it's actually the result of dealing with anger. There are different emotions and events that can trigger physical responses because these frequencies affect your organs.

John Assaraf

If I'm thinking positive thoughts, my brain is actually releasing the neurochemicals associated with those positive thoughts. So, we think about, "I'm thinking positive thoughts," and those neurochemicals are going into my bloodstream, and they're causing my cells to vibrate at the rate or vibration of the thought. If I think negative, sad, unhappy, limiting thoughts, those neurochemicals are going through my body. And this thing that we call our body is vibrating and oscillating at the level of the thoughts that we're thinking.

Dr. Steve Schwartz

Illness is all about an energetic disturbance in different parts of the body. And usually, as a diagnostic, the region where there is disease or dysfunction is the area where there is the most trauma. The disturbance trickles down into the physical body. So, if there was some kind of emotional trauma that happened from your parents or as a child, or you were bullied, or you had an extremely negative situation, that impression will get lodged in the cells as a vibrational resonance or a vibrational dissonance.

Jeremy Hoffmann

We have a physical body. We also have an energetic body. When there are things that are out of alignment, that are not tuned to the right frequencies in the energetic body, over a period of time, they can eventually begin to impact the physical body at a foundational level. When we hold onto anger, when we hold onto frustration, that energy will eventually get trapped in the physical body where it can manifest as tension, as dis-ease as other types of ailments, and they become something that we have to deal with.

> **"Life is not about finding yourself.
> Life is about creating yourself."**
>
> - George Bernard Shaw

"Keeping your body healthy is an expression of gratitude to the whole cosmos – the trees, the clouds, everything."

- Thich Nhat Hanh

PAST TRAUMA
CHAPTER FOUR

HEALING PAST TRAUMA

Baroness Dr. Kara Scott Dently

There's an entanglement within us that develops over time. You can become so focused your past that you're not able to move forward. Our natural form and desire is to *move forward*, but your mind, your body, your energy… everything about you wants to stay in the past because you're holding on to past memories.

Yet, we are here to move forward in time, particularly as everything else around us is moving forward. This resistance puts stress on your body. This is happening to a lot of people; they're storing this negative energy in their bodies, though they don't realize it, and it can show up as sickness.

Sir Dr. Antoine Chevalier

People who have unresolved issues from their childhood, sooner or later, will see these issues manifest as illness.

Every single criminal that I've treated, from schizophrenics and gang members to people who were criminally insane, had been sexually abused before the age of seven. That abuse is such a violation that they grow up unable to trust anyone; they feel completely on their own. And that level of rage, anger, and hate becomes translated into criminal behaviors and activities.

If you have that level of abuse before the age of seven, you might forget that it broke you; it essentially fractured your spirit and mind.

Morley Robbins

So many people have symptoms and they've just trained themselves to believe that their body is broken; they end up living their lives in fear. Now, in the short term, we can manage that. But, when they go into a *chronic* state of fear, a lifelong fear that they had done something wrong, and they can't make and mobilize their energy to respond positively to that stress, that's when symptoms show up.

Medice, Cura te Ipsum: *Physician, Heal Thyself*

- Luke 4:23

Sir James Gray Robinson, Esq.

You could be a miracle worker, but some people just won't heal, and there are several reasons for this. One is that they don't *believe* they can heal. Or, they have what's called a "secondary gain"; they're holding onto the illness because they're getting some kind of benefit from it. They're controlling their environment by making people wait on them hand and foot. And all of this is subconscious. Nobody *wants* to be sick, let alone terminally ill. However, their subconscious mind is so powerful that it will reject any energy that it senses is coming in that could change their current reality.

When you put your intention and your love into a signal, a projection into that person, that's where the healing comes from.

> **I have chosen to be happy because it is good for my health.**
>
> - Voltaire

Jason Estes

Energy work can be wonderful and healing. It can also be dangerous because you're coming to this space where you're not giving consent a lot of the time, especially in the new age movement. And so, what that does is it creates this violated feeling where there's no consent and because there is no consent to that, you're actually tearing holes in the field instead of strengthening it.

A lot of people who are getting this type of healing session are actually coming out worse than better. Now the opposite of that is when you *do get consent* and you're in that space where you're working together… that amplification causes amazing healing potential. I say potential because it's really up to you as the person to heal, based on whether or not you *want* to heal.

The biggest issue I think we have today with energy is that we don't realize the story is part of the reason. So, until you can let go of that story… whatever that story is, for whatever reason you're holding onto it, energy isn't going to change anything. It's just going to push up against it, making it harder for you.

Barbie Layton

Any fake kind of spirituality is something that can also be used for manipulation and power.

But, when you surrender yourself as a vehicle to be of service, beautiful things start to happen for you that you couldn't even imagine for yourself.

Sir Dr. Antoine Chevalier

In my humble opinion, people need a lot of assistance so they can actually connect with whatever false story is inside of them, and that will actually have the capacity to heal them. I have two PhDs and can call myself a doctor. However, I don't think of myself as a doctor or a healer. I choose to think of myself as just an assistant. I have knowledge; I can assist you. But the one who has the authority to *heal you* is you… your spirit.

Dr. Steve Schwatrz

When you go even deeper into a cell, you're operating at a different kind of physics; you're not operating at Newtonian physics… you're operating at quantum physics. And so, we think about a pathogen, like a bacterium, a virus, a parasite, a mold, fungus, yeast, or a mycoplasmal infection… any of these things… are more like energetic disturbances than they are an example of Newtonian physics. And that shift in perspective changes the way that we begin to look at the body and how to heal the body.

> **"The soul loves to meditate, for in contact with the Spirit lies its greatest joy."**
>
> - Paramahansa Yogananda

Morley Robbins

How do we cure fatigue? And how do we cure the penchant that we have to undermine our confidence in the fact that we have the natural ability to heal ourselves? We're all guilty of it.

The importance of empowerment, which is really what my whole focus is in, is to democratize healing. Get the individual back in control of their body. Give them a game plan but let them have the discretion to decide what to do and what not to do.

Dr. Steve Schwartz

Your disease state is highly organized in your physical body, which is so ironic because most people feel completely chaotic when in a diseased state.

But it's organized and it's vibrating at that level of dysfunction in your body.

So, if you want to heal that or reverse that, we need to disorganize the organization of that disease and essentially move you into a place of quantum… into a higher vibrational space… to allow your body to release and disorganize itself so it can align itself into a new dimensional reality. And this is the key of your choosing.

Sir Dr. Antoine Chevalier

There's only one requirement for this way to work. You have to want to be free from whatever that is. You have to want to be free from whatever you are aware of that you want to be free *from*. That's the only requirement, and that's what I call the law of intention. That's the most important.

It has to come from you, it has to come from that person, and then it can assist you and it will work. But, you really have to want to be free from whatever you're suffering from. Absolutely.

> **Heal me, oh Lord, and I shall be healed; save me, and I shall be saved. For thou art my praise.**
>
> - Jeremiah 17:14 [KJV]

Sir James Gray Robinson, Esq.

Fifty-one years ago, I fell off a four-story building and landed on a brick wall. And the way I hit it… I came down at an angle and I hit it with my hip, took out my left rib cage, and took off most of the left side of my face. And, I can only say that my soul bounced higher than my body because I remember distinctly looking down and watching people trying to resuscitate me.

The thing that was remarkable about that event is that the feeling and the awareness that I had when I was outside of my body was that I was not afraid; I didn't feel any pain. I was more curious as to what was going on and who was that body there on the ground. They say that miracles are for doubters and the slow-witted. I've had five of those events… so I must be one or the other. And the connection that I had, I believe, was with the divine. And all of that is kind of like a film on top of a glass that is your soul, your window to the divine.

Sir Dr. Antoine Chevalier

I had a case, a woman who was battling breast cancer. Obviously, breast cancer is physical, it's a physical manifestation. She was doing chemotherapy, radiation, and went through this multiple times for five years. She was able to actually defeat cancer every single time. Then, in a span of time of about every six to nine months in between, the cancer would come back… and come back… and come back.

So, finally, we had this session. She lied down on the bed and her eyes were closed and I assisted her. She went back in the past and it turns out when she was six years old, her mom said, "Well, your dad and I… we're going to separate; we're going to divorce. Who do you want to be with? Who do you want to live with?"

As a little girl, just six years old, at that moment in time, her heart got broken. She emotionally and physically got a broken heart. Later, in her sixties, that energy became heavier and heavier and became manifested in her physical body and in her heart. What is on top of her heart? The chest. And there, it manifested into breast cancer. When we discovered that, I assisted her to close the dimension of time, of that trauma at that moment of time when she was six years old and helped her to create a different memory of those events, one in which her heart didn't get broken. And, in a matter of three or four weeks, the blood work got better and she was cancer free. That was five years ago. She's still cancer free.

"Every patient carries her or his own doctor inside."

- Albert Schweitzer

"Success usually comes to those who are too busy to be looking for it."

- Henry David Thoreau

SUCCESS
CHAPTER FIVE

SUCCESS

Sir Don Boyer

Thomas Edison failed 10,000 times, we were told, when he was working on the electric light bulb. What caused him to keep going? What allowed him to maximize those failures and turn them into success and achievement?

When you begin to understand the world of energy and quantum physics, you understand and being to realize that you were born for success, you were designed and engineered for achievement. But, unfortunately, programmed for failure. When we understand this, we begin to get a glimpse of the power of energy and how we can harness that and move that into physical reality to create the success we want by the power of our thoughts and by changing our believe systems.

Attila Balazs

It means that every person desires to live a successful life. Everyone endeavors that. In order to be able to live a very successful life, it is important to have a value system and to have a goal with our own life. And it is important to believe in our goals. Belief is a very strong creative force.

> **"Success is the progressive realization of a worthy goal or ideal."**
>
> - Earl Nightingale

Eric Zehnder

Emerson said that most of the gifts we give to people are an excuse for not giving them ourselves. The best way I can say this is you are… and you are not. You have part of you've already developed and part of you is like, I'm waiting to become. Are you around the right people?

John Assaraf

Whenever we're looking at how to develop the mindset for achievement, the mindset for growth, first we have to understand that based on the science of neuroplasticity, the brain's ability to create and reinforce new patterns, we can shift what we believe to be true.

Whether we are worthy of success, whether we deserve to achieve success, whether we *can* achieve success, we can shift our habits of doing things the same way over and over again. So, what we want to do is ask ourselves, "What is it that we want to achieve - part one? Part two: What would I need to believe in order to make the achievement of this thing that I want to achieve more real?" Would I need to believe that I can learn what I need to learn?" Great, believe that! Would I need to believe that it's possible for me? Great believe that. So, we can choose our beliefs. And, in choosing our beliefs, we change the paradigm of how we see the world and how we see ourselves in the world achieving beliefs.

The other part of it is, "What can I do right now to achieve the goal?" The first part is to shift our perspective. And then, above all else, you have to take some inspired action consistently.

> **"Success is not how high you have climbed, but how you make a positive difference to the world."**
>
> - Roy T. Bennett

H.E. Baron Dr. John Sachtouras

Energy, and success… they go together. It is absolutely impossible to achieve any level of success without energy. You have to take action. Everything's down to the energetic level that we expose every day. Every single day, you see successful people say, "We take action, we get things done." Busy people say, "We always have time." Lazy people say, "Man, I have no time."

Sir James Gray Robinson, Esq.

Success is a pretty vague term. I think the most common definition of the word today is the ability to achieve success. It's not the goal; it's not the end result. It's the process. The thing that is important about energy and success is number one, forming the goal in the first place. What kind of energy created that goal? Was it positive energy like, "This will really help the world?"

Or is it negative energy like, "I'm broke. I'm starving and I need money?" That's what the difference is between positive and negative energy. Because if you have a negative mindset, you cannot achieve any goal. You will constantly sabotage yourself.

You have to be able to adopt a positive mindset in order to accomplish anything. You have to believe that you can do it. You have to believe that it's achievable. And, you have to believe that you can do it in one lifetime.

Attila Balazs

And with this reason, there is no successful or unsuccessful person, only a person with a positive or negative disposition.

So, the energy of a person with a positive attitude will represent a much higher level of success than the person with negative thinking.

> **"A positive mind finds a way it can be done; a negative mind looks for all the ways it can't be done."**
>
> - Napoleon Hill

Morley Robbins

What's really key to the labels of success and failure are a matter of perception. And the extent to which we think we have succeeded or failed is going to consume energy and it's going to have an effect on our ability to produce energy. But the whole notion of whether we did, in fact, succeed or did, in fact, fail, I think it's a lot safer to say that we're here to gain experience; we're here to learn.

And so, the perception of whether it is a success of failure is going to come with a price. There's going to be some impact that we have in terms of how we perceive ourselves, how we assess our performance, and we're going to need to be able to respond to that.

And the challenge is it's very easy to get caught in a loop and to begin to see patterns of success or patterns of failure. And then that becomes a very strong, emotional drain on the body.

Szilard Dosa

Energy is creating your results. You can notice it as success or you can notice it as failure. But, as a matter of fact, you are always successful because you always have the results of what you created. You don't need to know how the energy works to use it in your favor. I don't need to wait until I know everything, because I can use it now.

You can use your energy now to get anything you want in life.

"We are what we repeatedly do. Excellence, then, is not an act, but a habit."

- Aristotle

"In the end, it's not the years in your life that count; It's the life in your years."

- Abraham Lincoln

AWAKENING
CHAPTER SIX

If you want your creative people to reach the stars, give them space.

- Eric Zehnder

"Successful people are not without problems. They're simply people who've learned to solve their problems."

- Earl Nightingale

"Your opinion of yourself is your most important viewpoint. You are infinitely greater than you think you are."

- Neville Goddard

AWAKENING

Sir Don Boyer

When we look in the mirror, we believe that we are seeing ourselves, but are we? Actually, we are seeing our physical body and many people believe that's who they are. But, in reality, we are an energetic being… a spiritual being, that has no beginning and no ending. Our true spirit can never die.

Reality leaves a lot to the imagination.

- John Lennon

Dr. Steve Schwartz

We are physical manifestations of our own energetics. We are energy first and physical matter second.

Jeremy Hoffman

I believe that as humans, we are these little fractals, these fingers if you will, of energetic consciousness that is learning itself through our exploration, through our creativity, through our learning. We are here to respond, react, experience, swim in this field of energy.

Ultimately, there is no difference or separation between us and this consciousness that is energy. We are all swimming in this vast ocean that is energy. And we are all communicating with one another and with all things that are around us.

Eric Zehnder

I found the headwaters of the quantum river. I think that you have an energy flow in you, that your mind is separate from your brain. Your mind is language in that energy flow. The quantum river is energy. It's infinite.

The standard physics scientists have so much difficulty with quantum consciousness. It's a river. The moment your consciousness in a clear, clean way steps into it, it expands. The river gets bigger. You can never get outside the river. You can only go with it. Like the river is singular, you are singular, okay? You can't really get outside to look at yourself.

You have an identity. You are highly specific. What it takes to lift a specific identity out of a general background has got to be as big and as complex as the Universe itself.

Sir Dr. Antoine Chevalier

We are beings of energy. We are quantum beings, really. We are multidimensional spiritual beings, having a human experience. We are just scratching the surface.

> **"Feeling physically and mentally well is our own individual obligation."**
>
> - Andrew Huberman

Sir James Gray Robinson, Esq.

The power that we all possess that comes from our soul… I believe it's a connection to God… it is enormous. And that is one reason I do what I do today. And that's energy healing. Most quantum physicists will tell you that the Universe is expanding. And I believe that *we* are expanding. There's some fundamental code that we have inside of us.

Dr. Joe Vitale

So, sometimes people want to know, especially as they get older, is how does the awakening going beyond physical reality, going beyond the physical senses, play into the aging experience, to the dying experience.

As I sit here, I am… this is my 70th year, and I've had a long time to think about a lot of this and I'm still struggling with a lot of it. But here's something I've noticed.

The awareness of Joe that is here right now is the same awareness of Joe that was there when I was about five years old. I remember sitting on a chair wishing that my feet would be able to hit the floor. That memory is as alive in me now as it was then. And the person remembering it is the same one here. Yet I look at the outer body, well, obviously I hit the floor and I've aged in seven decades or so at this point. But, that awareness has remained consistent. I think that awareness is our spirit. I think that awareness of the spirit in me is the same spirit in you.

There is beyond the physical senses an unchanging energy source that is witnessing it all. So, when I go back in my memory and I remember being five years old and I'm this little kid sitting on the chair, and then my feet don't hit the ground and I'm wishing they would hit the ground; that energy source, the witness, was the one experiencing that.

When I went through high school, I was into boxing. At one point, I thought I was going to be heavyweight boxing champion of the world, so I transformed my body. I was the fittest I had ever been, and there was still the witness inside that was unchanged. That witness inside… that thing that was at peace… just noticed that Joe was going to be a boxer and Joe was doing all this.

As I'm sitting here in this moment, in present reality, that same still, small… it's not even a voice, but a still, small observer is observing.

"Hey, Joe's in another movie…" that's still small witness's probably still there. That's comforting, that's calming, that's serenity. And the more we can actually touch that, and come from that, and live from that, the more all of life works.

> **"Everyone has a watched life. Everyone is both the observer and the observed."**
>
> - Akiane Kramarik

Baroness Dr. Kara Scott Dentley

I'll tell you a story with my dad. My dad is no longer with us… I'll say it like that. He's with us but his physical body is no longer with us. But he received a diagnosis in 2021 that his heart was only functioning at 15%. And, for most people, that means no more life. They're pretty much writing you off at that point.

He understood something long ago. He would always, always tell us, "Sweet memories are forever." And now, I have a better, a more, a greater appreciation for those words.

I still feel his presence because I'm able to look at these memories of him. And I'm reminded that because of what we understand about energy and energy transfer, which is one that is actually the third law of thermodynamics, that energy is neither created nor destroyed; it's only transferred.

Morley Robbins

There is this natural intelligence in our body that knows where we are, how we're doing, what our needs are.

As a young boy, I had this… I guess it was an awakening or awareness that our purpose in life was to increase our consciousness, our creativity, and our compassion. That awareness became very powerful in my situation and drove me and it continues to drive me. And the awareness and the awakening that's evolved on a daily basis is absolutely mind blowing.

I start each day with one question: Where are we going today?

Dr. Joe Vitale

We don't need the whole world to be enlightened. That'd be fantastic if it happened. We need a significant percentage of the world, the people watching this, the people who are willing to do the meditations, the contemplations, to go into gratitude, to start acting from kindness, to listen to their inner guidance system, their own GPS. When all of that happens, they can bring a new level of awareness to the planet… a cleanse if you will.

And then a divine happening where there will be what I call "Heaven on Earth" will take place.

John Assaraf

I'll leave you with one final thought. Many, many years ago, Napoleon Hill brilliantly said, "Whatever the mind of man can conceive and believe, he can achieve." And our species has proven that to be true over and over again.

So now it's your turn.

"Your life does not get better by chance; it gets better by change."

- Jim Rohn

WITH GRATITUDE

Sir Don Boyer

As you and I have explored the world of quantum physics, we've looked at the depth of physical matter, and we've heard from experts from all over the world who have shared their wisdom, their understanding, and their experience.

As you've watched this journey begin to unfold, I trust that you gained a glimpse of how this life really works and have come to realize that you can be, do, and have *anything* that you desire.

I'm your host, Don Boyer. Thank you for being with me as we peered **beyond physical matter.**

"The unexamined life is not worth living."

- Socrates

This book is based on the film, "Beyond Physical Matter" a Motivate Production Film.

EXECUTIVE CREDITS, CAST, & CREW

LADY MELINDA BOYER
DIRECTOR

Melinda Boyer is an International Speaker, Author, and Film Director. She has authored several women's books, including *The Power of Mentorship for the Women Entrepreneur* and *The Power of Mentorship Women with Purpose*.

Melinda has also produced and directed more than nine documentaries including the Award-Winning film, *Beyond the Secret - The Awakening*. She has worked with some of today's top thought leaders, including Bob Proctor, Marie Diamond, Denis Waitley, Les Brown, John Assaraf, Carl Harvey, and Brian Tracy, among others.

Melinda and her husband Don are co-founders of the global mastermind group, "Carnegie Principle," which boasts a global membership. She is also focused on helping people raise their consciousness in order to create the life of their dreams.

www.MotivateEnterprise.com

SIR DON BOYER
PRODUCER/NARRATOR

Don Boyer is an international Speaker, Author, and Film Producer. He has authored more than twenty books and produced more than nine documentaries, including the award-winning film, *Beyond the Secret - The Awakening*.

Don has worked with some of today's top thought leaders, including Bob Proctor, Marie Diamond, Denis Waitley, Les Brown, John Assaraf, Carl Harvey, and Brian Tracy.

Along with his wife and business partner, Melinda, the couple co-founded the global mastermind group, "Carnegie Principle." As a Certified Intuitive Mentor, Don's clients include self-made millionaires, doctors, attorneys, professional sport figures, and celebrities. His focus lies in helping people to raise their consciousness so that they can create the life of their dreams.

www.MotivateEnterprise.com

SYLVAINE LANGLOIS
EXECUTIVE PRODUCER

Sylvaine Langlois has had a specialized nursing career for more than thirty-five years. She currently sits as an Influence Council member of the International Mastermind group, Carnegie Principle. She is also an owner and leader of the French Division of the Carnegie Principle.

Sylvaine is a published author, a founding member of Ascira, the company for the people. She is also an Executive Producer of international documentary movies along with some of the most influential people in the industry.

Her love, passion, and fascination for studying the Universal Laws has put her in the position to build lasting relationships and friendships with outstanding thought leaders from around the world. Her eagerness to learn and apply her knowledge of the Laws of the Universe has opened doors as if by magic. She knows it wasn't magic… but has simply been a matter of applying the right functioning of the Universal Laws.

Today, Sylvaine teaches and shares her knowledge to help people achieve their wildest dreams.

Mentor.Sylvaine@gmail.com
www.EliteTransformation.me

SIR JAMES GRAY ROBINSON, ESQ.

EXECUTIVE PRODUCER/CAST MEMBER

Sir James Gray Robinson, Esq. is an award-winning, third-generation trial attorney. After burning out in 2004, he quit practicing law and spent the next twenty years doing extensive research and innovative training to help others who are facing burnout or personal crises to heal.

He teaches wellness, transformation, and mindfulness internationally to thousands of private clients, businesses, and associations. Having experienced multiple near-death experiences has given him a deeper connection with divinity, understanding and spiritual energy. He has written over 14 books and has produced three documentaries to date.

www.JamesGrayRobinson.com

SIR SZILÁRD DÓSA
EXECUTIVE PRODUCER/CAST MEMBER

Sir Szilárd Dósa in a Mentor, Speaker, Author, Publisher, and the leader of the Hungarian Carnegie Principle. He is also an Executive Producer of the award-winning movies, *The Power of Thought, Beyond Limitation, and Beyond Physical Matter*. Ha has also been a featured expert in the movies *The Quest, Beyond Physical Matter and Beyond Mastermind Secret*.

He is a diligent student of Energy, Healing and Success for more than twenty years. He is a Certified Mentor, Ho'oponopono Practitioner, and Belief Clearing Practitioner.

He uses his gifts and talents to create and share teachings to help people awaken to their true self, let go the past, and to get into the true power.

Mentor@sirdosa.com
www.SirDosa.com

H.E. BARON DR. JOHN SACHTOURAS

EXECUTIVE PRODUCER/CAST MEMBER

H.E. Baron Dr. John Sachtouras is a vibrant entrepreneur and multi-lingual marketing strategist with more than four decades of solid and diverse professional experience in the areas of business development, principles of leadership, and teamwork.

He has owned, managed, and consulted for multi-million-dollar businesses in the USA and Latin America, for which he was responsible for everything from daily operations and corporate restructuring to strategic planning.

During his thirty plus years in network marketing, John has applied his experience, knowledge, and strategies to building organizations of more than one million global distributors, collectively producing more than a billion dollars in total revenue. His results have earned him tremendous personal and professional success. He is known as one of the most dynamic and influential leaders with some of the most significant organizational growth on record.

DUBAI: johnsach@gmail.com

SIR DR. ANTOINE CHEVALIER

EXECUTIVE PRODUCER/CAST MEMBER

Dr. Antoine Chevalier, PhD, HP, MPP, is an International Lecturer, Author, Researcher, and Functional Medicine Practitioner. In 2003, he was honored to accept a Knighting by the Royal Order of Constantine the Great and was also selected to receive the award of Top 100 Doctors in the World.

Dr. Chevalier holds two Ph.D.'s; one in International Sustainable Development and Anthropology and the other in Traditional Natural Healing Sciences. Along with top

Japanese Neurosurgeon Aya Nakano, MD, Ph.D., he is co-owner of the Nakano Clinic of Neurosurgery and their Japanese corporation "L'espoir" and Functional Medicine Clinic in Awaji Island, Japan.

Dr Chevalier is the proud recipient of the bronze medal from the prestigious organization "The Sons of American Revolution" for successfully treating more than 100 homeless, suicidal, PTSD, drug addict Veterans, and transitioning them from living in the streets into becoming productive members of society. He has also worked with gang members, autistic children, and sex trafficking survivors, as well as patients from all over the world suffering from a wide variety of illnesses.

www.a-Chevalier.com

JASON ESTES
EXECUTIVE PRODUCER/CAST MEMBER

Jason Estes is known as one of the leading Spiritual Teachers and pioneers of Quantum Field Technology. Emphasizing the importance of Self-Mastery, Total Responsibility, and clearing up the misunderstandings around True Wealth, one of Jason's main objectives is to provide free education that is accessible to all.

Jason is a Co-founder of Masters of the Void Organization (MTVO), whose requirement is "Authenticity at all costs." This is implemented during thousands of hours of coursework that drive those who feel called to test and cultivate ethics, integrity, and total responsibility. MTVO's purpose is to build the greatest living examples through cultivating Self-Mastery, which Jason says is "the single most important tool and the only thing that travels with us through Eternity."

Jason also co-founded Void Space Technologies, a tech company designed to bring stability, expansion, and support to the present with products that are divinely & ethically sourced. Jason believes that the future we will build is unlimited and empowered.

www.AlignedEarth.com
www.MTVO.org
www.EarthChange.com

TONY "DREAM MAKER" DODY

EXECUTIVE PRODUCER

Tony Dody is the Founder of the Dream Maker Agency. He is a "super connector" and mentor who works to bring people together to fulfill projects and help people's dreams come true.

He's a gifted communicator who has helped coach and mentor countless others to success, including top athletes, corporate executives, and the Hollywood elite. Tony focuses on the human connections that are integral to people being able to achieve their goals.

The Dream Maker has the vision to go beyond giving typical advice and, instead, offers his vast resources to help others realize their dreams.

JEFFREY LEVINE
EXECUTIVE PRODUCER

Jeffrey Levine holds a Bachelor of Science degree from the University of Hartford, Connecticut, a Juris Doctorate from the University of Mississippi Law School, and a Masters of Tax Law from Boston University.

Jeffrey is a frequent media guest for television and radio and has been featured in such magazines as *Kiplinger* and *Family Circle*. He has co- authored eight books including *Off The Radar* and *The Millionaire Frequency*. He's written a column for the Albany, New York Business Review for seventeen years and has been featured in several documentaries.

Some of his most notable achievements include helping a client become financially free by forty-five by taking his company public, he helped his clients ensure their financial security heading into retirement by negotiating a maximum sale for their dental practice, and has also helped various clients become millionaires in less than ten years. He's an avid philanthropist who has supported several organizations and funded scholarships for his local high school.

Jeff12levine@gmail.com

DR. MILTON HOWARD, JR.
MOVIE TRAILER MUSIC COMPOSER/CAST MEMBER

Dr. Milton Howard, Jr. is the founder of High-Definition Life, LLC (HD Life), which is leading the next generation of personal development. Milton Howard, Jr. has bridged the power of music and specific frequencies so that music has a more accurate impact upon the physiological state of an individual, therefore affecting their decision-making ability.

Milton has authored several books, workbooks, and children's books for HD Life and has produced music that lines up with the root causes of success and failure. These findings will change the world as people discover the truth about success and happiness. The human body is a system of rhythms and movements, and every human has a unique musical imprint just like their unique fingerprint.

Milton quit practicing law in 2004 to follow his true passion of healing. After 5 near death experiences, he developed an advanced connection with the divine and an ability to heal others. He has spent the last 19 years doing extensive research and innovative training to help others heal.

DR. STEVE SCHWARTZ

Dr. Steven Schwartz is a Chiropractor, visionary technology designer, sound alchemist, and regenerative medicine expert. He has been a pioneer in the advanced treatment of chronic illness, allergies, and emotional imbalances since 2000, exclusively using vibrational healing techniques and technologies.

Dr Schwartz is the founder of Bioharmonic Technologies and the creator of The VIBE System, which clears cellular memory and releases shock and trauma from the body.

He is also the author of *Primal Resonance, Discover the Secrets to Health, Vitality, and Optimal Human Performance,* in which he discusses the top ten ways to reverse aging and degeneration using sound, light, frequency, and vibration.

www.drstevenschwartz.com
info@bioharmonictechnologies.com

BARONESS DR. KARA SCOTT DENTLEY

Baroness Dr. Kara Scott-Dentley is a devoted wife to H.E. Baron Dr. James Dentley, and devoted mom to their son, Kaden. Prior to retiring at age 35, Kara served as a physicist and geospatial analyst for the United States Federal Government.

Among many notable accolades, Kara has received the Presidential Lifetime Achievement Award. Kara's research and publications have been recognized globally. She's also been featured in the *Women on the Move* television series. Kara's book, *Unlocking the Blueprint of Intention*, showcases her insights into unlocking personal greatness through the lens of science.

Dr. Kara founded the lifestyle brand, "L.I.F.E By Kara." Together, the Dentley's founded a non-profit organization "Already Always Amazing." They continue to serve many other organizations, including The Royal Order of Constantine the Great and Saint Helen.

www.LifebyKara.com
Lifebykara@gmail.com

ERIC ZEHNDER

Born on Camp Pendleton military base in California, Eric Zehnder came into this world with the love of language in his heart. This passion and its impact on both mind and spirit made Eric realize that it was his true Dharma to bring this gift into everyday life in a way that is relatable and moves people.

"The Quote-Master" has penned more than 20,000 original quotes, he shares that "science studies matter for answers; quantum physics studies energy for answers; I study language for answers, then I turn language into quotes." Eric produced another written work that took thirty years to write, entitled, *The River: Central Language Theory and Quantum Macro Physics*.

Eric shares, "I have JOY. Daily. Wave after wave. Once you taste it, you know instantly and forever you are NOT a machine. I can tell you how to get it. And QI - Quantum Intelligence - will outperform AI. Something as great as the discovery of the Americas is happening ON OUR WATCH. I hit a "Quantum River" of *exponential innovation*. It is the THRILL of your life. It is both super-intelligence and super-accelerative. It makes the heart bright and the mind brilliant.

He is the founder of Quantum River World and author of "Quantum Intelligence versus Artificial Intelligence."

www.QuantumRiverWorld.com

ATTILA BALAZS

Attila Balázs lives in Hungary. For more than thirty years, 30 years, he has trained hundreds of thousands of people in the areas of healthy lifestyle and financial culture. His companies have achieved million-dollar turnover.

His work is focused on helping people walk the path of health instead of illness so they can reach a physically, spiritually, mentally, and energetically fulfilled and healthy life, therefor eliminated disease. His main goal is to prepare people for the advent of the Golden Age and to raise health awareness to a higher level of consciousness.

ba@balazsattila.com
www.balazsattila.com

JOHN ASSARAF

John Assaraf is a world-renowned mindset and success expert who has appeared numerous times on Larry King Live, Anderson Cooper, and The Ellen DeGeneres Show.

He has built 5-multimillion-dollar companies, written two New York Times bestselling books and has appeared in 14 movies including the blockbuster hit "The Secret '' and "Quest For Success," with Richard Branson and the Dalai Lama.

He is passionate about helping people tap into their brain's superpower so they shatter limitations and achieve their life's biggest goals and dreams. John founded myNeuroGym.com, which is revolutionizing mindset coaching and mental fitness training. His powerful "Innercise app" helps people rewire their brain for unstoppable success.

www.MyNeurogym.com

JEREMY HOFFMANN

Jeremy J. Hoffmann is a passionate and impact-driven entrepreneur who reimagines the intersections of entertainment, wellness, and community by building intentional wellness experiences.

His homeschooled background has inspired him to unleash his out-of-the-box thinking to create change for millennials and Gen Z. Jeremy is driven by creating impact over profit while having as much fun as possible.

He has founded various companies, raised millions of dollars, and has won leadership awards. He's also developed specialty natural supplements. Join Jeremy on his socials and become part of his remarkable journey.

www.quantum.spa
@jeremyjhoffmann
Jeremy@Quantum.spa

DR. JOE VITALE

Dr. Joe Vitale is the globally famous and legendary author of numerous books, audios, courses and more.

He received the U.S. President Lifetime Achievement Award in 2024. Before that, in 2021, he won the Los Angeles Tribune Lifetime Achievement Award.

Joe starred in the blockbuster 2006 movie *The Secret* and he's got his own movie, "Zero Limits." Joe is also President of the Napoleon Hill Institute.

www.MrFire.com

MORLEY M. ROBBINS, MBA, CHC

Morley Robbins is a "retired" hospital executive and healthcare consultant who chose to become a Wellness Coach in 2009. In the process, he became a self-taught mineral expert. His highest purpose is to share his scientific research on the profound metabolic interplay between three key minerals: Magnesium, Bioavailable Copper, and Iron. These mineral-driven metabolic concepts are not fully understood, nor appreciated in practitioner circles, and are typically not yet in the public's consciousness.

In his quest to focus on mineral research and share his findings, he manages two websites to provide mineral education: The MAG Facebook Group, **www.GotMag.org** and The Root Cause Protocol, **www.theRootCauseProtocol.com.**

His primary focus is on mastering mineral metabolism and its foundational impact on our health.

Morley has devised a unique blood test to reveal these mineral dynamics, and he regularly trains practitioners to use this diagnostic tool in their practices. He has now performed over 5,500 consultations with clients in 45 countries around the world through his Copernican Institute.

www.theRootCauseProtocol.com
www.GotMag.org

BARBIE LAYTON

Barbie Layton is a scientifically verified Quantum Healer, Speaker, Bestselling Author, and Executive Coach. Her mission is to empower CEOs, elite athletes, and individuals to discover self-love, reinvigorate their dreams, and become the true VIPs of their lives. Barbie holds an M.A. in Spiritual Psychology from the University of Santa Monica.

Her personal journey has been marked by five near-death experiences, a battle with chronic illness, and other significant traumas. Barbie used these challenges to dedicate herself to healing and serving others.

She's been featured in national media including *USA Today, Wildmag,* and *Forbes.* Barbie also played a counseling role in the award-winning documentary, *The Prison Project*, which was centered around Viktor Fankl's work.

www.BarbieLayton.com

Special thanks to the following
For their support in the production of

BEYOND PHYSICAL MATTER

SPONSORS:

- JD3TV
- H.E. Baron Dr. John Sachtouras
- Carnegie Principle
- Awakened Mastery, Inc.

Special Thanks:

- Lisa Winston
- Eric Zehnder

Production Facilities

- Milestone Media
- FILM2VIDEO.com

Camera

- Jacob Foglio

Film Editor

- Andrew Hernandez

Motivate Enterprise, Inc.

Beyond Physical Matter, The Book
Transcription, Editing

- Robin Jay

MOTIVATE ENTERPRISE INC.

www.ingramcontent.com/pod-product-compliance
Lightning Source LLC
Chambersburg PA
CBHW050913160426
43194CB00011B/2393